ESSENTIALS

FOR LIFE

CREATED BY TIERCE GREEN

GOOD FEED
MEDIA

ESSENTIALS FOR LIFE

Published by Good Feed Media

ISBN: 979-8-9921538-0-4

This book supports the video content created and presented by Tierce Green. There are eight sessions in the series. Each session is about 30 minutes, including the main teaching and personal stories.

Video sessions for this series are completely FREE within the **Good Feed Media** App. There is no obligation to pay anything, but you have the opportunity to help us KEEP IT FREE by paying it forward.

Order additional copies of this resource and high-definition videos of the series for public viewing from Good Feed Media.

GOOD FEED MEDIA

FREE APP. FREE CONTENT.

ORDER RESOURCES AND DOWNLOAD THE APP AT GOODFEEDMEDIA.COM

Good Feed Media is a division of Tierce Green Ministries, Inc.

Video production by Layne Laughter.

Cover photo by Andrew Neel on Unsplash.

Distributed by:

Tierce Green Ministries, Inc.
The Woodlands, TX
tiercegreen.com

CONTENTS

ABOUT THE CONTENT

The central focus of **Essentials For Life is** on **3 Essential Relationships**:

Devotion To God
Sessions 2, 3, and 4

Community With Believers
Sessions 5 and 6

Influence With Others
Session 7

A fundamental principle in **Essentials** is that the best environment to work out our salvation and develop our faith is in community with other imperfect believers. We need a safe place with no condemnation but lots of accountability.

Watching the sessions alone is a less-than experience. The best practice is to go through this series with others and process the principles together. You need the encouragement and perspective of others. And others need the same from you.

Video sessions of this content can be freely accessed on the Good Feed Media App. Learn more and download at GOODFEEDMEDIA.COM

ABOUT THE AUTHOR

Tierce Green has over 45 years of professional ministry experience, including 30 years as a full-time speaker for conferences and retreats and 15 years of local church ministry. He served as a Student Pastor in a church of 1,200 and an Executive Pastor in a church of 12,000, where he led over a thousand men each week for seven years in a seasonal gathering called The Quest in The Woodlands, Texas.

Tierce is on the presentation team of **33 The Series** for Authentic Manhood, which has reached over three million men worldwide. He is the Director of **Authentic Manhood Initiative**, coaching leaders to reach men with the principles of biblical manhood. He is also the Director of **Good Feed Media**, creating quality disciple-making content like this that is freely available on the Good Feed Media App.

Tierce and his wife, Dana, have one daughter, Anna, and live in The Woodlands, TX.

1

FOUNDATION AND FRAMEWORK

3 ESSENTIAL RELATIONSHIPS

I. INTRODUCTION

A. Quality of Life is a big deal in our culture.

1. What is Quality of Life?

- "An individual's perception of their position in life in the context of the culture and value systems in which they live and in relation to their goals, expectations, standards, and concerns."[1]

2. How would you rate your Quality of Life on a scale of 1 to 10?

3. Our values determine the grid we use to measure Quality of Life.

- How we measure our Quality of Life continues to define our values.

- It's a cycle: Your input—what you read or watch and who you subscribe to—feeds your perspective. Then, your perspective drives what you read or watch and who you subscribe to.

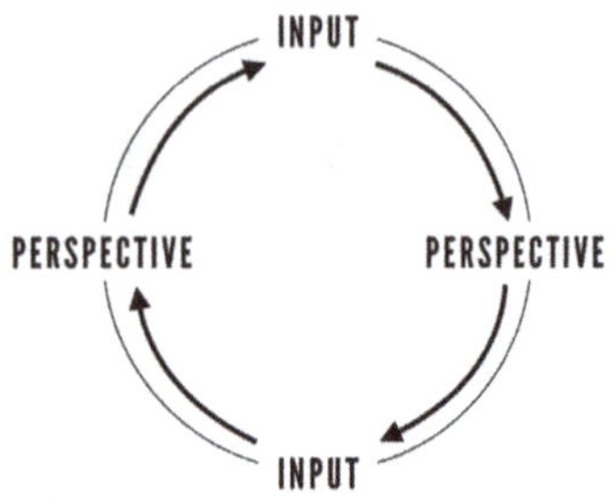

4. One of the most debilitating practices: The tendency to constantly compare ourselves with what we perceive to be the reality of others.

- Many of us experience a general disappointment with life.

[1] The World Health Organization Quality of Life (WHOQOL), 2012, p.11

B. A compelling promise made by Jesus:

- John 10:10b // I have come that they may have life, and have it to the full. (NIV)

- The quality of life Jesus promised is in a category all to itself.

II. OUR FOUNDATION IS JESUS

A. His credentials:

1. Jesus is God.

   - John 1:1-3 // In the beginning was the Word, and the Word was with God, and the Word was God. He was with God in the beginning. Through him all things were made; without him nothing was made that has been made. (NIV)

   - John 1:14 // The Word became flesh and made his dwelling among us. We have seen his glory, the glory of the one and only Son, who came from the Father, full of grace and truth. (NIV)

2. Jesus is the life.

   - John 14:6 // I am the way and the truth and the life. No one comes to the Father except through me. (NIV)

B. We're not seeking a better quality of life. We're seeking Jesus who is the life.

- 1 John 5:12 // Whoever has the Son has life; whoever does not have the Son of God does not have life. (NIV)

III. OUR FRAMEWORK: 3 ESSENTIAL RELATIONSHIPS

A. The Greatest Commandments

- Jesus made it clear that our life should center on loving God and loving others. When asked, "What is the greatest, or most important, commandment?" this was His answer:

  - Matthew 22:37-40 // Love the Lord your God with all your heart and with all your soul and with all your mind. This is the first and greatest commandment. And the second is like it: Love your neighbor as yourself. All the Law and the Prophets hang on these two commandments. (NIV)

B. Love God and Love Others

C. These two commandments give us *3 Essential Relationships: Devotion To God, Community With Believers,* and *Influence With Others.*

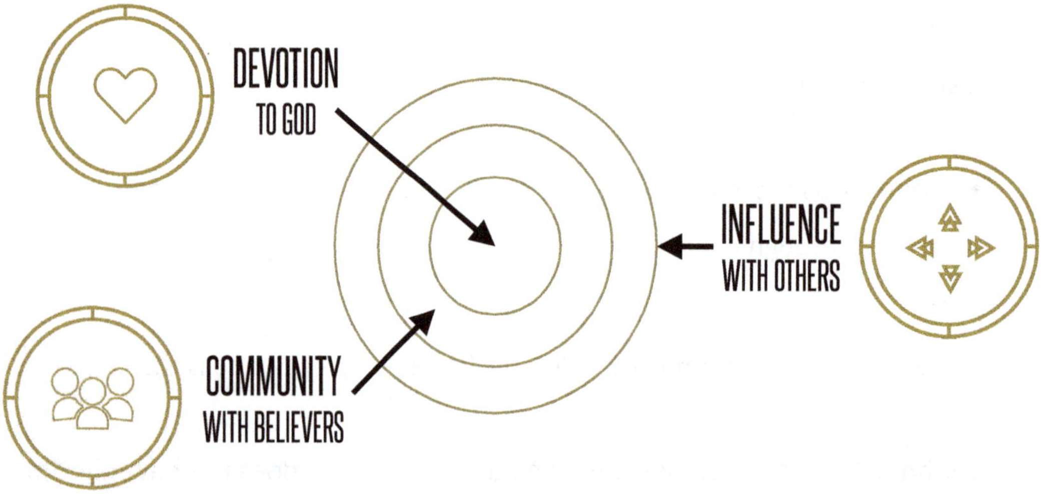

IV. MEASURING QUALITY OF LIFE

A. Are you becoming more like Jesus?

- Romans 8:29-30 // God knew what he was doing from the very beginning. He decided from the outset to shape the lives of those who love him along the same lines as the life of his Son ... We see the original and intended shape of our lives there in him ... (MSG)

B. Are you bearing spiritual fruit?

- Galatians 5:22-23 // But the fruit of the Spirit is love, joy, peace, patience, kindness, goodness, faithfulness, gentleness, and self-control ... (ESV)

C. Are you learning to feed yourself?

- Hebrews 5:12-13 // In fact, though by this time you ought to be teachers, you need someone to teach you the elementary truths of God's word all over again. You need milk, not solid food! Anyone who lives on milk, being still an infant, is not acquainted with the teaching about righteousness. (NIV)

D. Are you daily choosing to follow Jesus?

- There is no such thing as microwave maturity.

- Luke 9:23 // If anyone would come after me, he must deny himself and take up his cross daily and follow me. (NIV)

E. Are you disciplined?

- 1 Corinthians 9:27 // I discipline my body and keep it under control, lest after preaching to others I myself should be disqualified. (ESV)

F. Are you doing what God's Word says?

- James 1:22 // Do not merely listen to the word, and so deceive yourselves. Do what it says. (NIV)

G. Is there a measurable difference in your relationships, values, and goals?

V. A TRUE FOLLOWER OF JESUS

A. We can't experience the life Jesus promised without God's grace.

- We need Jesus because He is the life.
- 1 John 5:12 // He who has the Son has life; he who does not have the Son of God does not have life. (NIV)
- Religion without a relationship with God is dead.

B. The Very Bad News

- Romans 3:23 // All have sinned and fall short of the glory of God. (NIV)

- Romans 6:23 // The wages of sin is death, but the gift of God is eternal life in Christ Jesus our Lord. (NIV)

- Hebrews 9:22 // The law requires that nearly everything be cleansed with blood, and without the shedding of blood there is no forgiveness. (NIV)

C. The Very Good News

- Romans 5:8 // God demonstrates his own love for us in this: While we were still sinners, Christ died for us. (NIV)

D. How can this become your story?

- Romans 10:9-10 // If you declare with your mouth, "Jesus is Lord," and believe in your heart that God raised him from the dead, you will be saved. For it is with your heart that you believe and are justified, and it is with your mouth that you profess your faith and are saved. (NIV)

- Pray in your own words and with a sincere heart. Then, ask God to help you live like you mean it. You won't be perfect, but by God's grace, you will see a measurable difference. Remember God's promise: "He who has the Son has life!"

VI. CONCLUSION

A. OUR FOUNDATION: An authentic relationship with God through Jesus.

B. OUR FRAMEWORK: ***3 Essential Relationships: Devotion To God, Community With Believers,*** and ***Influence With Others.***

TALK ABOUT IT

1. How have you understood this promise from Jesus: ***I have come that they may have life and have it to the full?***

2. How do you think your life compares to the quality of life others are experiencing?

3. What values do you use to determine your quality of life? Have those values changed through the years? If so, how?

4. Look at the seven questions for MEASURING QUALITY OF LIFE on pages 9-10. In which areas do you see progress? Which areas need work?

5. How has God's grace made a measurable difference in your life? What's your story?

NOTES

NOTES

2

DEVOTION TO GOD

COMMUNICATION WITH GOD

I. INTRODUCTION & REVIEW

A. Welcome back to Essentials For Life!

- Everything in this series centers around ***3 Essential Relationships: Devotion To God, Community With Believers,*** and ***Influence With Others.***

B. There's no such thing as microwave maturity.

- Cultivating the best things that are full, meaningful, satisfying, and lasting takes time.
- Galatians 6:7-9 // Do not be deceived: God cannot be mocked. A man reaps what he sows. Whoever sows to please their flesh, from the flesh will reap destruction; whoever sows to please the Spirit, from the Spirit will reap eternal life. Let us not become weary in doing good, for at the proper time we will reap a harvest if we do not give up. (NIV)

II. SOME OF THE BEST SEEDS YOU CAN SOW ARE THE SEEDS OF PRAYER

A. Our relationship with God started with prayer.

- We prayed and received His grace.
- We prayed and surrendered our life to His authority.

B. Of all the things Jesus did, prayer is the one thing His disciples specifically asked Him to teach them how to do.

- Luke 11:1 // One day Jesus was praying in a certain place. When he finished, one of his disciples said to him, "Lord, teach us to pray." (NIV)

C. Prayer is intended to be open and honest communication with God.

III. WHAT DID JESUS TEACH ABOUT PRAYER?

A. Don't try to impress God or others.

- Matthew 6:5 // And when you pray, do not be like the hypocrites, for they love to pray standing in the synagogues and on the street corners to be seen by others. Truly I tell you, they have received their reward in full. (NIV)

B. Avoid meaningless repetition.

- Matthew 6:7 // And when you pray, do not keep on babbling like pagans, for they think they will be heard because of their many words. (NIV)

C. Pray in secret.

- When you pray, go into your room, close the door and pray to your Father who is unseen. Then your Father, who sees what is done in secret will reward you. (Matthew 6:6, NIV)

D. Pray in Jesus' name.

- John 14:14 // You may ask for anything in my name, and I will do it. (NIV)

IV. PRACTICAL TIPS

A. Pray through each day's plans.

- Proverbs 16:3 // Commit to the Lord whatever you do, and he will establish your plans. (NIV)

B. Keep a prayer journal.

- 1 Chronicles 16:12 // Remember the wonders He has done ... (NIV)

C. The ACTS of Prayer.

- **A** = ADORATION: adoring and worshiping God.
- **C** = CONFESSION: asking God's forgiveness for specific sins.
- **T** = THANKSGIVING: thanking God for what He has done.
  - 1 Thessalonians 5:18 // Give thanks in all circumstances; for this is God's will for you in Christ Jesus. (NIV)
- **S** = SUPPLICATION: asking God to supply our needs.
  - Philippians 4:6 // Do not be anxious about anything, but in everything by prayer and supplication with thanksgiving let your requests be made known to God. (ESV)

V. WHEN IT SEEMS LIKE GOD ISN'T LISTENING

A. Four Questions:

1. Am I praying with the right motives?

- James 4:3 // When you ask, you do not receive, because you ask with wrong motives, that you may spend what you get on your pleasures. (NIV)

2. Am I praying with humility?

- James 4:6 // God opposes the proud but gives grace to the humble. (NIV)

3. Is there hidden sin in my life?

- Psalms 66:18 // If I had cherished sin in my heart, the Lord would not have listened. (NIV)

4. Do I have an unforgiving heart?

- Matthew 6:14-15 // For if you forgive other people when they sin against you, your heavenly Father will also forgive you. But if you do not forgive others their sins, your Father will not forgive your sins. (NIV)

B. How do we remove the hindrances to prayer and open the communication channels?

- James 4:8 // Draw near to God, and He will draw near to you. (ESV)

VI. WHEN WE DON'T KNOW WHAT TO PRAY

A. Romans 8:26-27 // In the same way, the Spirit helps us in our weakness. **We do not know what we ought to pray for**, but the Spirit himself intercedes for us through wordless groans. And he who searches our hearts knows the mind of the Spirit, because the Spirit intercedes for God's people in accordance with the will of God. (NIV)

B. Some of the best prayers are prayers without words when we listen, let the Holy Spirit intercede, and let God do what only He can do.

VII. CONCLUSION

A. Any meaningful relationship requires good communication, especially our relationship with God.

B. Open and honest communication with God will help you love Him more deeply and others more tangibly.

TALK ABOUT IT

1. What were some of the prayers you heard or prayed as a child? (bedtime, mealtime, etc.)
2. How do you feel about praying out loud in a group or a public gathering? What about praying out loud with your family?
3. How has God answered your prayers? Have you had any unexpected answers?
4. Look at the ACTS of Prayer on page 16. Which of the four parts need work in your life?
5. Look at the four questions for WHEN IT SEEMS LIKE GOD ISN'T LISTENING on page 19. Have any of those been a struggle for you?
6. Talk about a time when circumstances were so hard you didn't know what to pray. How did God lead you through that time as you prayed?

NOTES

NOTES

3

DEVOTION TO GOD

BUILDING GOD'S WORD INTO YOUR LIFE

I. INTRODUCTION

A. As a follower of Jesus, we need reliable directions.

- We need a clear picture of who Jesus is, and we need to hear from Him.

B. God's Word is the most reliable life-map there is.

- When we build God's Word into our lives, the Holy Spirit will access its truth and use it to direct us.
- John 14:26 // The Holy Spirit, whom the Father will send in my name, will teach you all things and will remind you of everything I have said to you. (NIV)

C. Too often, we want to hear a word ***from*** God, but we don't want to read the Word ***of*** God—or maybe we don't know how to read it.

The decline of the knowledge of the holy has brought on our troubles. A rediscovery of the majesty of God will go a long way toward curing them. It is impossible to keep our moral practices sound and our inward attitudes right while our idea of God is erroneous or inadequate. If we would bring back spiritual power to our lives, we must think of God more nearly as He is.[2] – A.W. Tozer

[2] A.W. Tozer, *The Knowledge of the Holy*

II. 3 THINGS WE NEED TO KNOW ABOUT GOD'S WORD:

A. God has revealed Himself in His Word.

B. God's Word is timeless and personal.

- We need to shift our passion from just studying the Bible to knowing God.
- Bible knowledge alone can become a smokescreen that hides what's really going on inside our hearts.
    - Matthew 23:27-28 // Woe to you, teachers of the law and Pharisees, you hypocrites! You are like whitewashed tombs, which look beautiful on the outside but on the inside are full of the bones of the dead and everything unclean. In the same way, on the outside you appear to people as righteous but on the inside, you are full of hypocrisy and wickedness. (NIV)

C. The goal is transformation.

- Romans 12:2 // Do not conform to the pattern of this world, but be transformed by the renewing of your mind. Then you will be able to test and approve what God's will is—his good, pleasing and perfect will. (NIV)
- If the information stops in our head, we're no more than a modern-day Pharisee. If it stops in our heart, we're just a fanatic. When it makes it to our hands and feet, we're a true disciple.

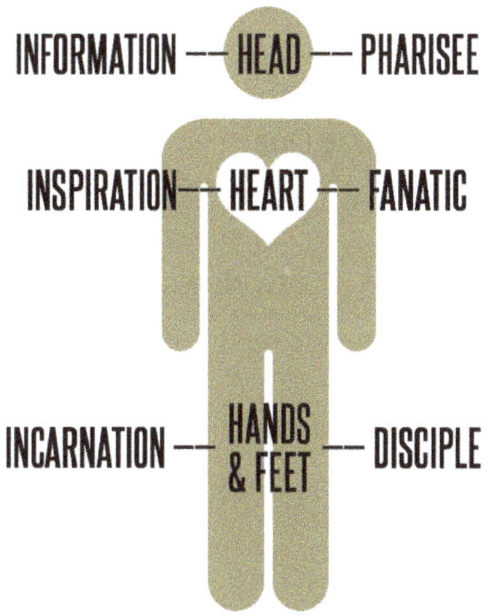

III. 3 SIMPLE QUESTIONS:

A. What is the Timely Message?

B. What is the Timeless Principle?

C. What is the Personal Application?

IV. HOW DO YOU GET STARTED?

A. Purchase a notebook or journal.

B. Choose a short book.

C. Check your attitude.

- Reverence, expectancy, and a willingness to obey.

D. Day One:

- Slow down and be still. Take time to focus and prepare your heart.
- Read 5-10 verses or until a thought seems to be complete—typically a paragraph or two. There aren't any rules to this. Just read a short section that makes sense to you.

- In your notebook or journal, record the date and the scripture reference.

- Write down your thoughts about what you read. You can write as much as you want or as little as you want. At least write down some things you want to pray about.

- Conclude your time by praying about what God has shown you in His Word and praying about the things on your list.

E. Day Two and beyond:

- Begin reading where you left off the day before and repeat the process.

- After a week or two, you'll begin to see an improvement in the way you hear God speak to you as you build His Word into your life.

V. MEDITATING ON SCRIPTURE

Matthew 4:4 // Man shall not live on bread alone, but on every word that comes from the mouth of God. (NIV)

A. Meditation changes the way we act by changing the way we think.

- Romans 12:2a // Do not conform to the pattern of this world, but be transformed by the renewing of your mind ... (NIV)

B. 5 Practical Benefits of Meditating on God's Word:

Joshua 1:8 // Keep this Book of the Law always on your lips; meditate on it day and night, so that you may be careful to do everything written in it. Then you will be prosperous and successful. (NIV)

1. Meditation equips us to follow through with our faith.

2. Meditation enables us to be prosperous and successful.

    - The promises in Joshua 1:8 are conditional. IF we meditate on God's Word, THEN we'll be able "to do everything written in it." IF we meditate on God's Word, THEN we'll be prosperous and successful.

3. Meditation recalibrates our prayers.

    - John 15:7 // If you remain in me and my words remain in you, ask whatever you wish, and it will be done for you. (NIV)

4. Meditation helps us sin less.

    - Psalm 119:11 // I have hidden your Word in my heart that I might not sin against you. (NIV)

5. Meditation provides specific directions for life.

    - Psalm 119:105 // Your word is a lamp for my feet, a light on my path. (NIV)

C. How do we meditate on scripture?

1. Meditation starts with memorization.

    - If we treasure God's Word and use it regularly, we're highly motivated and much more likely to memorize it.

- Proverbs 7:2-3 // Guard my words as your most precious possession. Write them down, and also keep them deep within your heart. (LB)

- Psalm 119:72 // The law from your mouth is more precious to me than thousands of pieces of silver and gold. (NIV)

2. Memorize it, then personalize it.

   - Put it in your own words. Make it personal by replacing the pronouns in the verse with your name.

3. Pray it.

   - As you pray, look for ways to integrate God's personalized truth into your open and honest communication with Him.

VI. CONCLUSION

A. The Apostle Paul outlined the high value of Scripture in his letter to a young leader named Timothy.

   - 2 Timothy 3:16-17 // All Scripture is God-breathed and is useful for teaching, rebuking, correcting and training in righteousness, so that the servant of God may be thoroughly equipped for every good work. (NIV)

B. God's Word teaches and trains us. Sometimes it rebukes and corrects us. It equips us. And to be thoroughly equipped, we need to build it into our life.

TALK ABOUT IT

1. Which phrase describes your experience with God's Word: ***a love/hate relationship; I never read a verse I didn't like; I appreciate it but rarely read it; hard to understand.***
2. What has God's Word revealed to you about God Himself?
3. What are some of your go-to scriptures that give you encouragement and strength?
4. Look through the content in this workbook. Pick some scriptures that resonate with you that you think would be helpful to add to your memorize and meditate list.
5. If transformation is the goal, how has God's Word been used to transform your life? How has it trained you, corrected you, and equipped you?

BIBLE STUDY RESOURCES

- **Bible Study Fellowship** – In-depth Bible studies with trained group leaders for all ages and denominations worldwide. Learn more at bsfinternational.org.
- **Precept** – Since 1970, Precept has been equipping small group Bible Study Leaders who can help you discover the truth of Scripture for yourself. Learn more at precept.org.
- **The Bible Recap** – A chronological reading plan that follows the story of Scripture as the events occurred. This one-year plan corresponds to The Bible Recap podcast (available wherever you listen to podcasts) Learn more at thebiblerecap.com
- **The Navigator Bible Study Handbook** – Learn how to do question-and-answer studies, verse analysis studies, comprehensive chapter analysis studies, and topical studies.
- **Rick Warren's Bible Study Methods** – 12 different Bible study methods to help you explore biblical truths, apply them to your life, and grow as a disciple.
- **Study Bibles**
  - The New Inductive Study Bible
  - Life Application Study Bible
- **My Utmost for His Highest** — A timeless devotional book by Oswald Chambers. This is not a pure Bible study book, but it is an effective change-up to keep our eyes fixed on Jesus.

NOTES

NOTES

4

DEVOTION TO GOD

SEEKING GOD WITH ALL YOUR HEART

I. INTRODUCTION & REVIEW

A. We identified *Devotion To God* as the first of *3 Essential Relationships*.

- It's first on our list because Jesus said it was first on His list.

  - Matthew 22:37-38 // Love the Lord your God with all your heart and with all your soul and with all your mind. This is the first and greatest commandment. (NIV)

B. Communication with God and building His Word into our life are vital to developing our *Devotion To God*.

- Our objective is to know and love God.

- Even when we have the right purpose and the right motivation, there are times when life can get out of balance and out of focus. There are times when we don't know where to turn, and we have no clue what our next move should be.

- Comfort and hope:

  - Jeremiah 29:11-13 // "For I know the plans I have for you," declares the Lord, "plans to prosper you and not to harm you, plans to give you hope and a future. Then you will call on me and come and pray to me, and I will listen to you. You will seek me and find me when you seek me with all your heart." (NIV)

  - This passage adjusts our aim from seeking God's plans to seeking Him—from seeking God's will to seeking God.

C. God promises that we will find Him when we seek Him with all our heart.

II. WHAT DOES IT MEAN TO SEEK GOD WITH ALL YOUR HEART?

A. It starts with our values. We passionately pursue what we value the most.

- Matthew 13:44-46 // The kingdom of heaven is like treasure hidden in a field. When a man found it, he hid it again, and then in his joy went and sold all he had and bought that field.

  Again, the kingdom of heaven is like a merchant looking for fine pearls. When he found one of great value, he went away and sold everything he had and bought it. (NIV)

B. There's a difference between seeking God's hand and seeking His face.

- When you seek His hand, you're primarily interested in what He can do for you.

- When you seek His face, you're longing for Him, not just His blessings.

  - Psalm 27:8 // You have said, "Seek my face." My heart says to you, "Your face, Lord, do I seek." (NIV)

III. THE CHALLENGE TO SEEK GOD WITH ALL OUR HEART APPEARS THROUGHOUT THE SCRIPTURES.

- Psalm 119:2 // Blessed are those who keep his statutes and seek him with all their heart. (NIV)

- Psalm 105:4 // Look to the Lord and his strength; seek his face always. (NIV)

- Proverbs 3:5-6 // Trust in the Lord with all your heart, and do not lean on your own understanding. In all your ways acknowledge him, and he will make straight your paths. (ESV)
- Psalm 37:4 // Delight yourself in the Lord, and he will give you the desires of your heart. (ESV)
- Isaiah 26:9 // My soul yearns for you in the night; in the morning my spirit longs for you. (NIV)
- Psalm 63:1 // O God, you are my God; earnestly I seek you; my soul thirsts for you; my flesh faints for you, as in a dry and weary land where there is no water. (NIV)
- Matthew 5:6 // Blessed are those who hunger and thirst for righteousness, for they shall be satisfied. (ESV)

IV. ONE OF THE MOST EFFECTIVE WAYS TO SEEK GOD WITH ALL YOUR HEART IS FASTING.

A. Spiritual fasting typically involves replacing food with prayer for a designated period.

B. The cravings are our cue to seek God with all our heart.

C. The most beneficial fast for some of us could be a technology fast.

D. We fast because the value of eternal things is greater than the value of temporary things.

E. We fast because we want to be better positioned to know God and better conditioned to be used by Him.

Prayer is the one hand with which we grasp the Invisible; fasting the other, with which we let loose and cast away the visible. – Andrew Murray

F. In Matthew 6:16, Jesus implies that fasting will be a regular practice in the lives of His followers. He says, "When you fast," not "If you fast."

Jesus takes it for granted that His disciples will observe the pious custom of fasting. Strict exercise of self-control is an essential feature of the Christian life. Such customs have only one purpose—to make the disciples more ready and cheerful to accomplish those things which God would have done.

– Dietrich Bonhoeffer, *The Cost of Discipleship*

V. BIBLICAL EXAMPLES

A. Moses fasted before he received the Ten Commandments from God.

- Deuteronomy 9:9 // When I went up the mountain to receive the tablets of stone, the tablets of the covenant that the Lord made with you, I remained on the mountain forty days and forty nights. I neither ate bread nor drank water. (NIV)

B. King David fasted and prayed that God would spare the son he had conceived from an adulterous relationship with Bathsheba.

C. Daniel fasted after receiving a troubling vision from God.

- Daniel 10:2-3 // In those days I, Daniel, was mourning for three weeks. I ate no delicacies, no meat or wine entered my mouth, nor did I anoint myself at all, for the full three weeks. (NIV)

D. After Jesus was baptized, He fasted to prepare for His public ministry.

- Matthew 4:1-2 // Then Jesus was led up by the Spirit into the wilderness to be tempted by the devil. And after fasting forty days and forty nights, he was hungry. (NIV)

E. After a personal encounter with the resurrected Jesus on the Damascus Road, Saul, now called Paul, fasted.

- Acts 9:9 // For three days he was without sight, and neither ate nor drank. (NIV)

- Those three days of fasting could have been a mix of being in shock, repenting, and preparing for the uncertainty of what was next.

NOTE: Fasting is not intended to be a rigid religious ritual with specific instructions and restrictions that must be followed. The objective is to seek God with all our heart and get in sync with His will and purpose for our life.

VI. WHEN SHOULD WE FAST?

A. When a new ministry or mission is about to begin.

- Acts 13:2-3 // While they were worshiping the Lord and fasting, the Holy Spirit said, "Set apart for me Barnabas and Saul for the work to which I have called them." So after they had fasted and prayed, they placed their hands on them and sent them off. (NIV)

B. When the odds against us are great.

- Judges 20 captures the story of the Israelites losing 22,000 in battle on one day and 18,000 in battle the next day. Finally, we see a shift in verse 26:

  - Judges 20:26; 28 // Then the Israelites ... went up to Bethel, and there they sat weeping before the Lord. They fasted that day until evening ... The Lord responded, “Go, for tomorrow I will give them into your hands.” (NIV)

C. When the confession of sin requires it.

- 1 Samuel 7:6 // On that day they fasted and there they confessed, “We have sinned against the Lord.” (NIV)

D. When we want to amp up our worship.

- Luke 2 tells the story of an 84-year-old prophetess named Anna.

  - Luke 2:37 // ... She never left the temple but worshiped night and day, fasting and praying. (NIV)

VII. HOW SHOULD WE FAST?

A. Jesus makes it clear that we should fast the same way we pray—to connect with God, not to impress others.

When you practice some appetite-denying discipline to better concentrate on God, don’t make a production out of it ... If you “go into training” inwardly, act normal outwardly. Shampoo and comb your hair, brush your teeth, wash your face. God doesn’t require attention-getting devices. He won’t overlook what you are doing. He will reward you well. – Matthew 6:16-18, *The Message*

VIII. HOW DO WE GET STARTED?

A. Choose something you value.

B. Set aside an appropriate range of time to abstain from the thing you choose.

C. Focus on God, not on the fast.

- The goal is not to make it through the fast, but to connect with God on a more intimate level, to seek Him with all your heart.
- The Fast Test: (1) Do you love God more deeply? (2) Do you love others more tangibly?

TALK ABOUT IT

1. What is something you wanted so desperately that you sacrificed to get it? What obstacles did you encounter? What adjustments did you make to acquire it?
2. How much of the time do you seek God's face compared to seeking His hand?
3. What are some ways you seek His face?
4. Have you ever fasted for physical reasons? Describe the circumstances and outcome.
5. Have you ever fasted for spiritual reasons? Describe the circumstances and outcome.

NOTES

NOTES

5

COMMUNITY WITH BELIEVERS

BENEFITS OF A CONNECTED LIFE

I. INTRODUCTION & REVIEW

A. Our objective is not to seek a better quality of life but to seek Jesus, who is the life.

- 1 John 5:12 // Whoever has the Son has life; whoever does not have the Son of God does not have life. (NIV)

B. The framework for this series comes from Matthew 22. When one of the experts in religious law asked Jesus, "What is the greatest, or most important, commandment?" He clarified the essence of God's will and purpose for our life:

- Matthew 22:37-39 // Jesus replied: "'Love the Lord your God with all your heart and with all your soul and with all your mind.' This is the first and greatest commandment. And the second is like it: 'Love your neighbor as yourself.'" (NIV)

C. From these two commandments—Love God and Love Others—we identified ***3 Essential Relationships: Devotion To God, Community With Believers,*** and ***Influence With Others***. All three are vital for a full and meaningful life.

D. The last three sessions focused on our ***Devotion To God.*** We talked about prayer, which is open and honest communication with God. We learned how to build God's Word into our life and what it looks like to seek God with all our heart.

E. The second ***Essential Relationship*** is ***Community With Believers***.

II. 4 THINGS WE NEED TO KNOW ABOUT COMMUNITY WITH BELIEVERS:

A. Our relationship with God gives us a relationship with each other.

- Our connection with each other was initiated by God and accomplished through Jesus.
    - John 1:11-13 // He came to that which was his own, but his own did not receive him. Yet to all who did receive him, to those who believed in his name, he gave the right to become children of God—children born not of natural descent, nor of human decision or a husband's will, but born of God. (NIV)

B. We are a community of imperfect believers.

- There is a difference between our ***position*** in Christ and our ***performance*** as believers.
- There will always be a disparity between our position and our performance.
- The challenge is to close the gap.
    - Philippians 2:12 // ... continue to work out your salvation with fear and trembling. (NIV)
- The best place to do this is in authentic community with believers.

That is what God has called the church to be about: creating environments where authentic community can take place. Building relational, transforming communities where people are experiencing oneness with God and oneness with one another. Communities that are so satisfying, so unique, and so compelling that they create thirst in a watching world.[3] – Andy Stanley and Bill Willits

[3] Andy Stanley and Bill Willits, Creating Community: ***5 Keys to Building a Small Group Culture*** (Multnomah, 2004), 45.

C. Most people settle for less.

- We have hundreds of social media connections that we call "friends" but are not really known by anyone.

- God says this is not good.

    - Genesis 2:18 // It is not good for the man to be alone ... (NIV)

D. God created us for authentic community.

- It's in these environments that our human-shaped void is filled.

- We need a safe place with people we trust—a place where there's no condemnation but lots of accountability.

III. 5 DEGREES OF COMMUNICATION: [4]

A. The Cliché Level

- It's "How's it goin'?" without really wanting to know the answer. It's "What do you think about this weather?" No real connection, just clichés.

B. The Fact Level

- Acquaintance-level exchanges. The fact level holds people at arm's length. It doesn't let them in.

---

[4] John Powell, ***Why Am I Afraid to Tell You Who I Am?***

C. The Opinion Level

- You share what you think, but you're still keeping people at a safe distance. It's somewhat satisfying because you've contributed to the conversation.

D. The Emotional Level

- Now you're beginning to give away who you are. At this level, you're conveying your hopes and fears, your disappointments and defeats.

E. The Transparent Level

- Transparency is genuine and powerful. When you practice healthy transparency with a true friend, they will be drawn to you rather than driven away.

- 1 Corinthians 10:13a // No temptation has overtaken you except what is common to mankind ... (NIV)

True friendship begins when one person says to another, "What? You, too? I thought I was the only one." – C.S. Lewis

IV. 6 BENEFITS OF A CONNECTED LIFE:

A. Authentic community sharpens us.

- Proverbs 27:17 // As iron sharpens iron, so one person sharpens another. (NIV)

B. Authentic community helps us connect on a soul level.

- 1 Samuel 18:1 // ... the soul of Jonathan was knit to the soul of David, and Jonathan loved him as himself. (NIV)

C. Authentic community can provide wisdom for making good decisions.

- Proverbs 15:22 // Plans fail for lack of counsel, but with many advisors they succeed. (NIV)

D. Authentic community provides mutual encouragement.

- Hebrews 10:24-25 // And let us consider how to stir up one another to love and good works, not neglecting to meet together, as is the habit of some, but encouraging one another, and all the more as you see the Day drawing near. (ESV)

E. Authentic community provides protection.

- 1 Peter 5:8 // Be alert and of sober mind. Your enemy the devil prowls around like a roaring lion looking for someone to devour. (NIV)

- 1 Corinthians 10:13 // ... God is faithful; he will not let you be tempted beyond what you can bear. But when you are tempted, he will also provide a way out so that you can endure it. (NIV)

F. Authentic community provides comfort when life hurts.

- 1 Corinthians 12:26 // ... If one part suffers, all the other parts suffer with it ... (NIV)

- Romans 12:15 // Rejoice with those who rejoice; mourn with those who mourn. (NIV)

- God designed us to laugh with each other in the good times, walk with each other in the tough times, and hold each other in the terrible times.

- Ecclesiastes 4:9-10 // Two are better than one ... If one falls down, his friend can help him up. But pity the man who falls and has no one to help him up! (NIV)

V. CONCLUSION

A. Community With Believers is vital to our spiritual development and even our emotional and physical well-being.

B. Start with the connections you already have.

- Share your story with someone you trust.

- Improve your chances to cultivate soul-level connections.

    - Join groups built around Bible Study, common missions, shared interests, or seasons of life.

C. Community With Believers provides proof to the world of who Jesus is.

- John 13:34-35 // A new command I give you: Love one another. As I have loved you, so you must love one another. By this everyone will know that you are my disciples, if you love one another. (NIV)

TALK ABOUT IT

1. How can understanding the difference between our ***position*** in Christ and our ***performance*** as followers of Jesus help us build community with believers?

2. We're all works in progress. How has community with believers sharpened you and encouraged you as a follower of Jesus?

3. How has authentic community protected you from making a mistake or rescued you when you did?

4. How has authentic community provided comfort when you were going through a difficult time?

5. Who are your soul-level connections? With whom do you feel safe to be transparent?

NOTES

NOTES

6

COMMUNITY WITH BELIEVERS

BLESSINGS OF A GENEROUS LIFE

I. INTRODUCTION

A. A snapshot of the church in its infancy.

- Acts 2:42-47 // They devoted themselves to the apostles' teaching and to fellowship, to the breaking of bread and to prayer. Everyone was filled with awe at the many wonders and signs performed by the apostles. All the believers were together and had everything in common. They sold property and possessions to give to anyone who had need. Every day they continued to meet together in the temple courts. They broke bread in their homes and ate together with glad and sincere hearts, praising God and enjoying the favor of all the people. And the Lord added to their number daily those who were being saved. (NIV)

B. Details of their story:

- They were building God's Word into their lives.
- Prayer was an active part of their culture.
- They functioned as a body.
- They were seeking God with all their heart.
- The news of what was going on was influencing others.

C. Generosity doesn't come naturally.

II. 5 THINGS WE NEED TO KNOW ABOUT GENEROSITY

A. Our generosity reflects God's generosity.

- John 3:16 // For God so loved the world that he gave his one and only Son, that whoever believes in him shall not perish but have eternal life. (NIV)

B. Generosity strengthens our faith.

- Proverbs 3:9-10 // Honor the Lord from your wealth and from the first of all your produce; Then your barns will be filled with plenty, and your vats will overflow with new wine. (NASB)

- Luke 6:38 // Give and it will be given to you ... For by your standard of measure, it will be measured to you in return. (NASB)

C. Generosity is the antidote for materialism.

- 1 Timothy 6:17-19 // Command those who are rich in this present world not to be arrogant nor to put their hope in wealth, which is so uncertain, but to put their hope in God, who richly provides us with everything for our enjoyment. Command them to do good, to be rich in good deeds, and to be generous and willing to share. In this way they will lay up treasure for themselves as a firm foundation for the coming age, so that they may take hold of the life that is truly life. (NIV)

D. Generosity blesses us in return.

- Proverbs 11:25 // A generous man will prosper; he who refreshes others will himself be refreshed. (NIV)

E. Generosity is an investment in eternity.

- Matthew 6:20 // Store up for yourselves treasures in heaven, where moth and rust do not destroy, and where thieves do not break in and steal. (NASB).

III. GENEROSITY IS IMPORTANT TO GOD

A. We invest in what we really believe in.

- Matthew 6:21 // Where your treasure is, there your heart will be also. (NIV)

B. Generosity reveals the depth of our Devotion To God and the strength of our Community With Believers.

C. The goal is not tithing but to develop a life of generosity.

- 2 Corinthians 8:7 // Just as you excel in everything—in faith, in speech, in knowledge, in complete earnestness, and in your love for us—see that you also excel in the grace of giving. (NIV)

- The word we translate as "excel" implies to super-abound and to exceed a fixed number or measure.

IV. UNDERSTANDING THE PURPOSE OF THE TITHE

A. The word "tithe" simply means a tenth part.

B. Examples of tithing before Mosaic Law:

- Genesis 14 // Abraham and Melchizedek
- Genesis 28 // Jacob
- The nature of each act was voluntary, not out of compulsion. Their heart was in it, and ten percent seemed to be a reasonable expression of their devotion to God.

C. Tithing under Mosaic Law

- There were at least three tithes that the Israelites were required to give:
  - One-tenth of the produce of their land and livestock to support the Levitical priesthood.
  - A tithe for the festivals.
  - A tithe for the poor over seven farming years.
- The tithing rate at times could have been as high as 22 to 30 percent.

D. Is tithing relevant today?

- Matthew 5:17 // Do not think that I have come to abolish the Law or the Prophets; I have not come to abolish them but to fulfill them. (NIV)

  - The word "fulfill" means that all the requirements of the Law are complete in Jesus. This is the New Covenant, but it doesn't invalidate the Old Testament.

- We have a different motivation for obedience that flows from a grateful heart that's being transformed by the Holy Spirit.

  - Under the New Covenant, tithing has been expanded and reshaped. It includes a number of transformative principles that extend beyond giving ten percent of your income to potentially giving much more.

  - The question is not, "What percentage am I required to give?" Instead, and this is a radical question, "What percentage of my heart have I given to God?"

V. 3 LEVELS OF GIVING [5]

A. **Spontaneous Givers** are emotionally driven.

B. **Strategic Givers** plan ahead so they can be really generous.

C. **Sacrificial Givers** see possessions as tools that God provides for us to advance his kingdom on earth.

[5] Craig Groeschel, ***Weird: Because Normal Isn't Working***

VI. THE CURSE OF AN UNGENEROUS LIFE

A. Opting out of a generous life is like stealing from God.

- Malachi 3:8-9 // Will a man rob God? Yet you rob me. But you ask, "How do we rob you?" In tithes and offerings ... You are under a curse—the whole nation of you—because you are robbing me. (NIV)

- An ungenerous life puts us under a curse.

B. Undoing the curse.

- Malachi 3:10 // Bring the whole tithe into the storehouse ... "Test me in this," says the Lord Almighty, "and see if I will not throw open the floodgates of heaven and pour out so much blessing that there will not be room enough to store it." (NIV)

- Start by giving at least ten percent to your "storehouse" (your church—your local community of believers).

- If you can't do that, commit what you can and then stretch a little more.

C. Remember: Jesus has completely fulfilled all the requirements of the Law.

- You don't have to do any of this.

- Why wouldn't you at least want to tithe, just out of gratitude and worship for what Jesus has done for you?

VII. CONCLUSION

A. We can't afford to be ungenerous.

B. Start with the 80/10/10 Plan: 10% to God, 10% to savings, and 80% to live on. Then stretch yourself to live on less so you can give and save more.

C. You may need help with a plan to get out of debt. It will take discipline, but God will help you. All discipline is hard, but you'll be healthier because of it.

D. A lesson from Jesus:

- Luke 21:3-4 // "Truly I tell you," he said, "this poor widow has put in more than all the others. All these people gave their gifts out of their wealth, but she out of her poverty put in all she had to live on." (NIV)

- A comfortable offering for those who have lots of money may look like a huge offering to others.

- The widow gave all she had. That's sacrificial giving.

- God measures generosity not by the amount that is given but by the sacrifice.

E. Don't get hung up on the tithe.

- The challenge is to exceed a fixed number or measure—to excel in the grace of giving — and reflect God's extreme generosity.

- Matthew 10:8 // Freely you have received, freely give. (NIV)

OUR LOVE FOR GOD AND OTHERS CAN BE MEASURED: Not by ***what*** we give but ***how*** we give it. Not by the amount of the ***offering*** but by the ***sacrifice***.

TALK ABOUT IT

1. Do you think understanding that Jesus has fulfilled all the requirements of the Law will make people more or less likely to give generously?

2. When did you first learn about the practice of tithing? Was it communicated as more of a "have to" or "want to"?

3. Where are you on the 3 LEVELS OF GIVING SCALE:

SPONTANEOUS — STRATEGIC — SACRIFICIAL

1 2 3 4 5 6 7 8 9 10

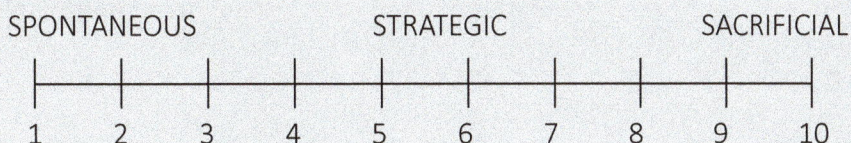

4. Who or what has inspired you to want to give generously?

5. How has developing a life of generosity strengthened your faith?

NOTES

7

INFLUENCE WITH OTHERS

WHO IS YOUR NEIGHBOR?

I. INTRODUCTION

A. In this session, we'll learn about the third ***Essential Relationship: Influence With Others.***

B. Who are "the others"?

- To love your neighbor as yourself is bigger than just your ***Community With Believers.***
- Each of us needs to ask the question: "Who is my neighbor?"

C. If we're not careful, our ***Community With Believers*** can become an isolated subculture.

- What Jesus taught and practiced was the opposite of that.
- Jesus was called a friend of sinners.

II. 4 STORIES

A. **STORY #1: The Parable of the Good Samaritan (Luke 10)**

- An "expert in the law" asked Jesus a direct question: "What must I do to inherit eternal life?" Jesus responded to his question with two questions: "What is written in the Law? How do you read it?"
- The man's answer was technically correct according to his faith.

- Luke 10:27-28 // "Love the Lord your God with all your heart and with all your soul and with all your strength and with all your mind," and "Love your neighbor as yourself."

  "You have answered correctly," Jesus replied. "Do this and you will live." (NIV)

- The "expert in the law" wanted to support his perspective.

  - Luke 10:29 // But he wanted to justify himself, so he asked Jesus, "And who is my neighbor?" (NIV)

- In the minds of the Jews, Samaritans were half-breeds, a less-than race of people.

- Jesus made the hero of the story a Samaritan.

  - Luke 10:36-37 // "Which of these three do you think was a neighbor to the man who fell into the hands of robbers?"

    The expert in the law replied, "The one who had mercy on him."

    Jesus told him, "Go and do likewise." (NIV)

B. STORY #2: Jesus and the Woman at the Well (John 4)

- John 4:9-10 // The Samaritan woman said to him, "You are a Jew and I am a Samaritan woman. How can you ask me for a drink?" (For Jews do not associate with Samaritans.)

  Jesus answered her, "If you knew the gift of God and who it is that asks you for a drink, you would have asked him and he would have given you living water." (NIV)

- This woman had five previous husbands and was currently living with a man she wasn't married to.

- Jesus didn't make her lifestyle the focal point of the conversation.
    - He talked about living water and what it truly means to worship God.
    - This woman was looking for answers to some of life's biggest questions.
    - When Jesus revealed who He was, it truly changed her life.

C. **STORY #3: Jesus and Simon the Pharisee (Luke 7)**

- An unexpected guest shows up with a costly jar of perfume.
    - She was described as a "woman of the city who was a sinner."
    - She weeps at the feet of Jesus, wetting His feet with her tears and wiping them with her hair. She pours the perfume on them and kisses His feet.
- Luke 7:39 // When the Pharisee who had invited him saw this, he said to himself, "If this man were a prophet, he would know who is touching him and what kind of woman she is—that she is a sinner." (NIV)
- Jesus knew quite well who she was.
    - He looked past her sin and saw her brokenness and the humility in her heart
    - Luke 7:48; 50 // Your sins are forgiven ... Your faith has saved you. Go in peace. (NIV)
- To the religious leaders, anyone who was a friend of sinners was a rebel.

D. STORY #4: Jesus and Zacchaeus (Luke 19)

- Zacchaeus was a Jew and an employee of the Roman Empire.
    - Tax collectors were notorious for increasing their fees beyond what was required and keeping the overage as personal profit.
    - Zacchaeus was a wealthy man, so he had accumulated a large amount of illegitimate wealth.
    - To the Jews in Jericho, Zacchaeus was a traitor.
- Zacchaeus climbed a tree so he could see over the crowd as they gathered around Jesus.
- Jesus suggested a safe place for Zacchaeus to get to know Him.
    - Zacchaeus was immediately grateful.
    - He gladly welcomed Jesus into his home.
- Luke 19:7 // All the people saw this and began to mutter, "He has gone to be the guest of a sinner." (NIV)
- Inside the home of Zacchaeus, we see a changed man.

III. GOD'S PLAN FOR THE CHURCH: GO INTO THE WORLD

A. Paul's message to the church in Philippi:

- Philippians 2:14-15 // Do everything without grumbling and arguing, so that you may be blameless and pure, children of God who are faultless in a crooked and perverted generation, among whom you shine like stars in the world. (HCSB)

B. Jesus proposed the same plan for influencing others:

- Matthew 5:16 // Let your light shine before others, so that they may see your good works and give glory to your Father who is in heaven. (ESV)

C. We put a light in places where it's dark.

IV. 6 THINGS TO HELP US HAVE AN EFFECTIVE INFLUENCE WITH OTHERS

A. Be confident about your identity.

- Our confidence is in what God has done for us.
- We were given the right to become God's children because we received Jesus; we accepted Him for who He is, our Savior and Lord.
- Jesus was confident in His identity, and our identity is in Jesus.

B. Be clear about the message.

- Keep your eye on the ball.
- The gospel is a message of grace and truth.

C. Learn to tell your story.

- There are three parts to your story:
  1. Your life before following Jesus.
  2. How you came to put your faith in Jesus.
  3. Your life as a follower of Jesus.
- Craft your story with others in mind.
  - Avoid clichés and phrases that only an insider would understand.
  - Be sure that our need for God's grace is clear.
- The more you tell your story, the better it will be, and the more confident you will be.

D. Be compassionate in the way you relate to others.

- 1 Peter 3:15 // Always be prepared to give an answer to everyone who asks you to give the reason for the hope that you have. But do this with gentleness and respect. (NIV)

- We need to see others not as targets to evangelize, but as people who need help.

- Matthew 9:36 // When he saw the crowds, he had compassion on them, because they were harassed and helpless, like sheep without a shepherd. (NIV)

- Sometimes it's more important to win the relationship instead of winning the the argument.

E. Create space for God to do what only He can do.

- We can point people to Jesus, but only God can change their hearts.

- Be patient and depend on the power of the Holy Spirit.

  - 1 Thessalonians 1:5 // Our gospel came to you not simply with words but also with power, with the Holy Spirit and deep conviction. You know how we lived among you for your sake. (NIV)

- Three things that create a healthy space for God to do what only He can do: words, reputation, and the power of the Holy Spirit.

F. Be courageous in your mission.

- Our fears seem unimportant compared to the dangers Paul faced.

  - 2 Corinthians 11:24-26 // Five times I received from the Jews the forty lashes minus one. Three times I was beaten with rods, once I was pelted with stones, three times I was shipwrecked, I spent a night and a day in the open sea, I have been constantly on the move. I have been in danger from rivers, in danger from bandits, in danger from my fellow Jews, in danger from Gentiles; in danger in the city, in danger in the country, in danger at sea; and in danger from false believers. (NIV)

- Remember what's really at stake: the souls of humanity.

V. CONCLUSION

A. Who is your neighbor? Who is in your circle of influence?

B. Loving your neighbor as yourself means being a friend like Jesus—a friend of sinners.

TALK ABOUT IT

1. Which of the 4 STORIES is the most compelling and challenging to you? (Pages 64-67: Good Samaritan, Woman at the Well, Simon the Pharisee, Zacchaeus)

2. In this session, we learned that God's plan has always been for us to go into the world and put a light in places where it's dark. What concerns do you have about being a true friend with people who aren't followers of Jesus?

3. Talk about your experience: (1) Followers of Jesus who became friends with you and helped you put your faith in Jesus, or (2) How God has been helping you be a friend to those who are not followers.

4. Pick a few people in your group to briefly share the three parts of their story (page 59):
    - Your life before following Jesus
    - A few details of how you came to put your faith in Jesus
    - A few details about your life since you became a follower

NOTES

8

A LIVING SACRIFICE

THE TOTAL PACKAGE

I. INTRODUCTION & REVIEW

A. We started this series with a compelling promise made by Jesus:

- John 10:10b // I have come that they may have life, and have it to the full. (NIV)

B. The preface to the promise explains why some people miss out on the life Jesus promised.

- John 10:10 // The thief comes only to steal and kill and destroy; I have come that they may have life, and have it to the full. (NIV)

C. Our primary objective is not to seek a certain quality of life but to seek Jesus, who is the life.

- 1 John 5:12 // Whoever has the Son has life; whoever does not have the Son of God does not have life. (NIV)

D. The best context for discovering God's will and purpose for our life is within the framework of ***3 Essential Relationships: Devotion To God, Community With Believers,*** and ***Influence With Others.***

E. The ***3 Essential Relationships*** should intersect.

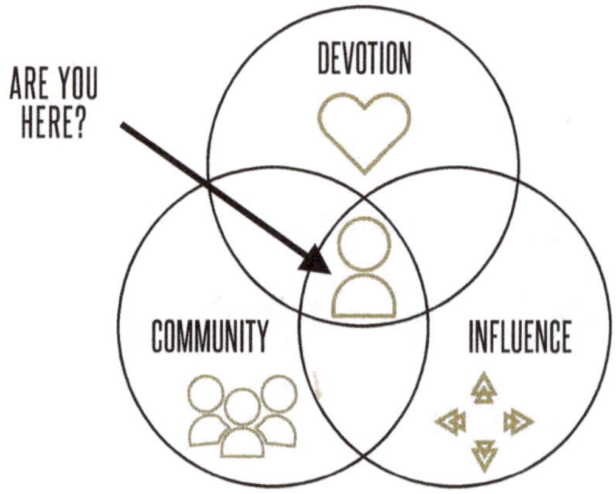

II. LIVING IN THE SWEET SPOT

A. Discipline keeps us in a better position for God to change us and in a better condition for God to use us.

B. The challenge to be a living sacrifice.

Therefore, I urge you, brothers and sisters, in view of God's mercy, to offer your bodies as a living sacrifice, holy and pleasing to God—this is your true and proper worship. Do not conform to the pattern of this world, but be transformed by the renewing of your mind. Then you will be able to test and approve what God's will is—his good, pleasing and perfect will. – Romans 12:1-2, NIV

III. WHAT IT LOOKS LIKE TO BE A LIVING SACRIFICE

A. We start with our position in Christ.

- "In view of God's mercy" reminds us that God gives us the right to be called His children.
- Our foundation is Jesus, and our motivation flows from God's mercy toward us.

B. Our reasonable response is unconditional surrender.

- 1 Corinthians 6:19 // Do you not know that your bodies are temples of the Holy Spirit, who is in you, whom you have received from God? You are not your own. (NIV)

- The total package: Love God with all our heart, soul, mind, and strength.

C. Our offering is dynamic and perpetual.

- Galatians 2:20 // I have been crucified with Christ and I no longer live, but Christ lives in me. The life I now live in the body, I live by faith in the Son of God, who loved me and gave himself for me. (NIV)

- This kind of sacrifice is "holy and pleasing to God."

D. We move into a different category of worship.

- This is our "true and proper worship."

- More than anything, God wants our heart.

- It recalibrates everything—the way we manage our time, our talents, and our treasures.

- 2 Corinthians 8:1-5 // And now, brothers and sisters, we want you to know about the grace that God has given the Macedonian churches. In the midst of a very severe trial, their overflowing joy and their extreme poverty welled up in rich generosity. For I testify that they gave as much as they were able, and even beyond their ability. Entirely on their own, they urgently pleaded with us for the privilege of sharing in this service to the Lord's people. And they exceeded our expectations: They gave themselves first of all to the Lord, and then by the will of God also to us. (NIV)

E. A living sacrifice is counter to the culture.

- Romans 12:2 juxtaposes what's happening in the world with what should be happening in our mind.

- Our mind is a battleground.

  - 2 Corinthians 10:5 // We demolish arguments and every pretension that sets itself up against the knowledge of God, and we take captive every thought to make it obedient to Christ. (NIV)

IV. THE PARADOX PRINCIPLE [6]

A. Die to live.

- Luke 9:23 // Whoever wants to be my disciple must deny themselves and take up their cross daily and follow me. (NIV)

- Paradox: "A seemingly absurd or self-contradictory statement or proposition that, when investigated or explained, may prove to be well-founded or true."

- A living sacrifice is a lifestyle—a daily practice—not a singular event.

B. The challenge in being a living sacrifice is to stay on the altar.

[6] *33 The Series, Volume 5: A Man and His Marriage* (Authentic Manhood, page 7)

C. A living sacrifice makes a measurable difference.

- Colossians 3:12-14 // ... Clothe yourselves with compassion, kindness, humility, gentleness and patience. Bear with each other and forgive one another if any of you has a grievance against someone. Forgive as the Lord forgave you. And over all these virtues put on love, which binds them all together in perfect unity. (NIV)

D. When you mess up, get back on the altar and remember your position in Christ.

- You look at life "in view of God's mercy."
- We run to the Father because we know He is gracious.

V. CONCLUSION – ISAIAH 6:1-8

A. God's holiness exposed Isaiah's sinfulness.

- Isaiah was humbled and broken.
- God initiated a solution, and Isaiah's sin was taken away.
- Isaiah 6:8 // "Here am I. Send me!" (NIV)
- Isaiah completely and unconditionally surrendered himself to God's will and purpose.

B. Are you a living sacrifice?

- Does God have access to every room in your heart?

- Renew your contract (your Devotion To God) daily.

    - Say "Yes, Lord!" and ask Him to start filling in the blanks.

- Go ALL IN with your heart, soul, mind, and strength—the total package.

TALK ABOUT IT

1. Are you living in the sweet spot where the ***3 Essential Relationships*** intersect? Which of the three are strong? Which are weak?

2. When you've made a mistake, are you more likely to try and cover it up, try and clean it up, or fall before Jesus and ask for His forgiveness and help?

3. What are your concerns about signing a blank contract with God?

4. Read Romans 12:1-2 again. Pray and ask God to help you go all in as a living sacrifice.

    Therefore, I urge you, brothers and sisters, in view of God's mercy, to offer your bodies as a living sacrifice, holy and pleasing to God—this is your true and proper worship. Do not conform to the pattern of this world, but be transformed by the renewing of your mind. Then you will be able to test and approve what God's will is—his good, pleasing and perfect will.

NOTES

ESSENTIAL MOVES

Information without application leads to frustration. Use this page to write down a few Essential Moves—personal steps you want to take to apply the principles from this series.

The goal is transformation, not behavior modification. The practice of writing down a plan with goals and steps will put you in a better position to experience God's purpose and the life Jesus promised.

Share your plan with trustworthy friends in authentic community with believers.

www.ingramcontent.com/pod-product-compliance
Lightning Source LLC
Chambersburg PA
CBHW081140090426
42736CB00018B/3428